HOLIDAY FUN

LUNAR NEW YEAR

KIM THOMPSON

Norwood House Press

Cataloging-in-Publication Data

Names: Thompson, Kim.
Title: Lunar New Year / Kim Thompson.
Description: Buffalo, NY : Norwood House Press, 2027. | Series: Holiday fun | Includes glossary and index.
Identifiers: ISBN 9781978580718 (pbk.) | ISBN 9781978580725 (library bound) | ISBN 9781978580732 (ebook)
Subjects: LCSH: Chinese New Year--Juvenile literature. | New Year--Juvenile literature. | Holidays--Asia--Juvenile literature. | Lunar calendars--Juvenile literature.
Classification: LCC GT4905.T548 2027 | DDC 394.261--dc23

Published in 2027 by
Norwood House Press
2544 Clinton Street
Buffalo, NY 14224

Designer: Rhea Magaro
Editor: Tricia Hoffman

Photo credits: Cover, p. 1 satawat nuntasiri/Shutterstock.com; p. 5 cowardlion/Shutterstock.com; p. 6 Bento Orlando/Shutterstock.com; p. 9 Kadagan/Shutterstock.com; p. 11 Prostock-studio/Shutterstock.com; p. 12 Maria Castellanos/Shutterstock.com; p. 15 japansainlook/Shutterstock.com; p. 16 Padodo/Shutterstock.com; p. 19 Carlos Huang/Shutterstock.com; p. 20 Dragon Images/Shutterstock.com; p. 21 CandyRetriever/Shutterstock.com;

Printed in the United States of America

Some of the images in this book illustrate individuals who are models. The depictions do not imply actual situations or events.

CPSIA compliance information: Batch #CSNHP27: For further information contact Norwood House Press at 1-800-237-9932.

TABLE OF CONTENTS

A NEW YEAR IS HERE!

A giant dragon puppet slithers by. Fireworks light the sky.

On this **holiday**, people say goodbye to the old. They welcome the new. It is **Lunar** New Year!

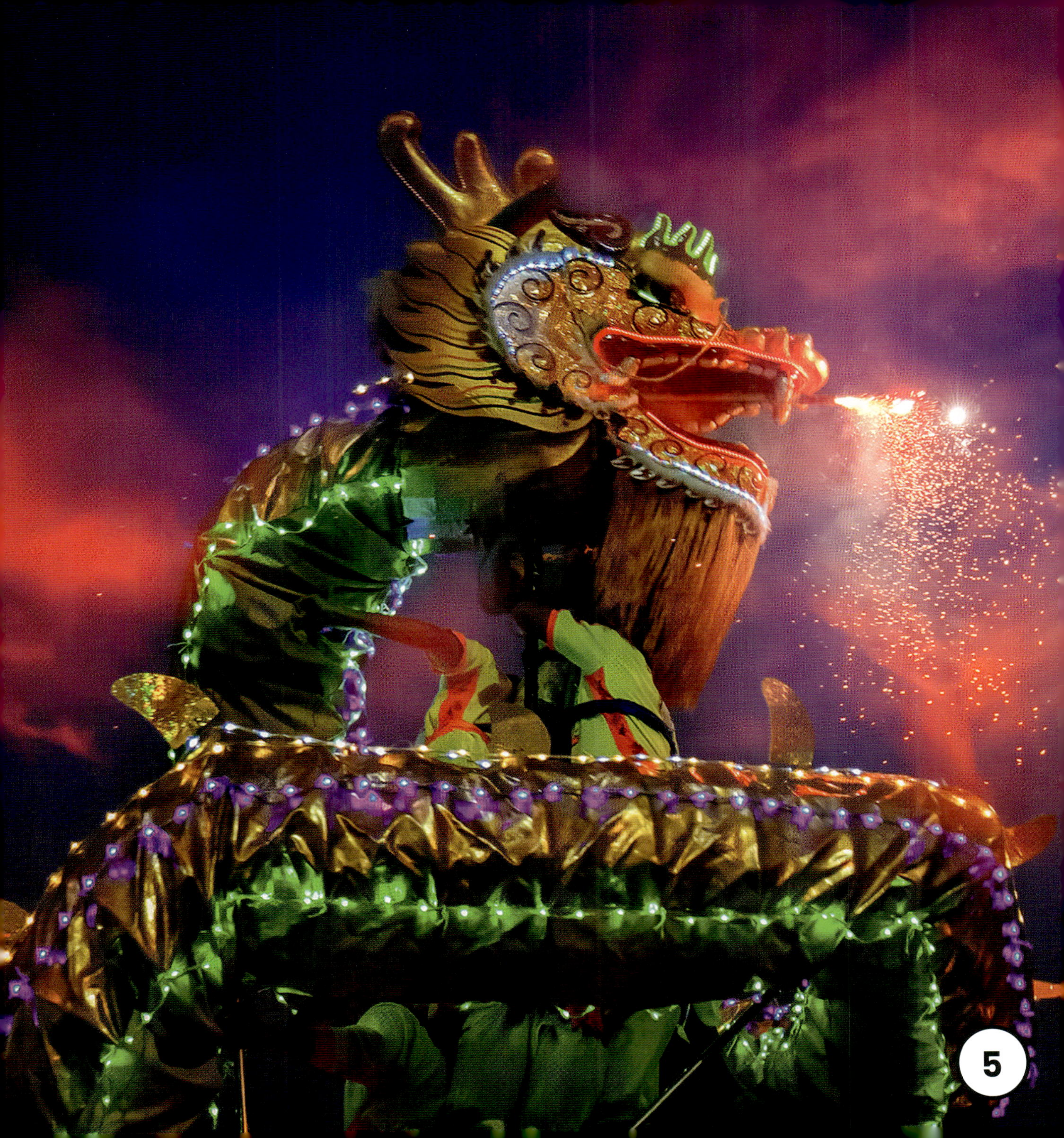

A SPECIAL TIME

Lunar New Year comes every year. It lasts for 15 days in January or February. A special calendar is based on the sun and moon. It tells when a new year starts. The holiday begins the same day.

Each year gets an animal name. The year 2027 is the Year of the Goat.

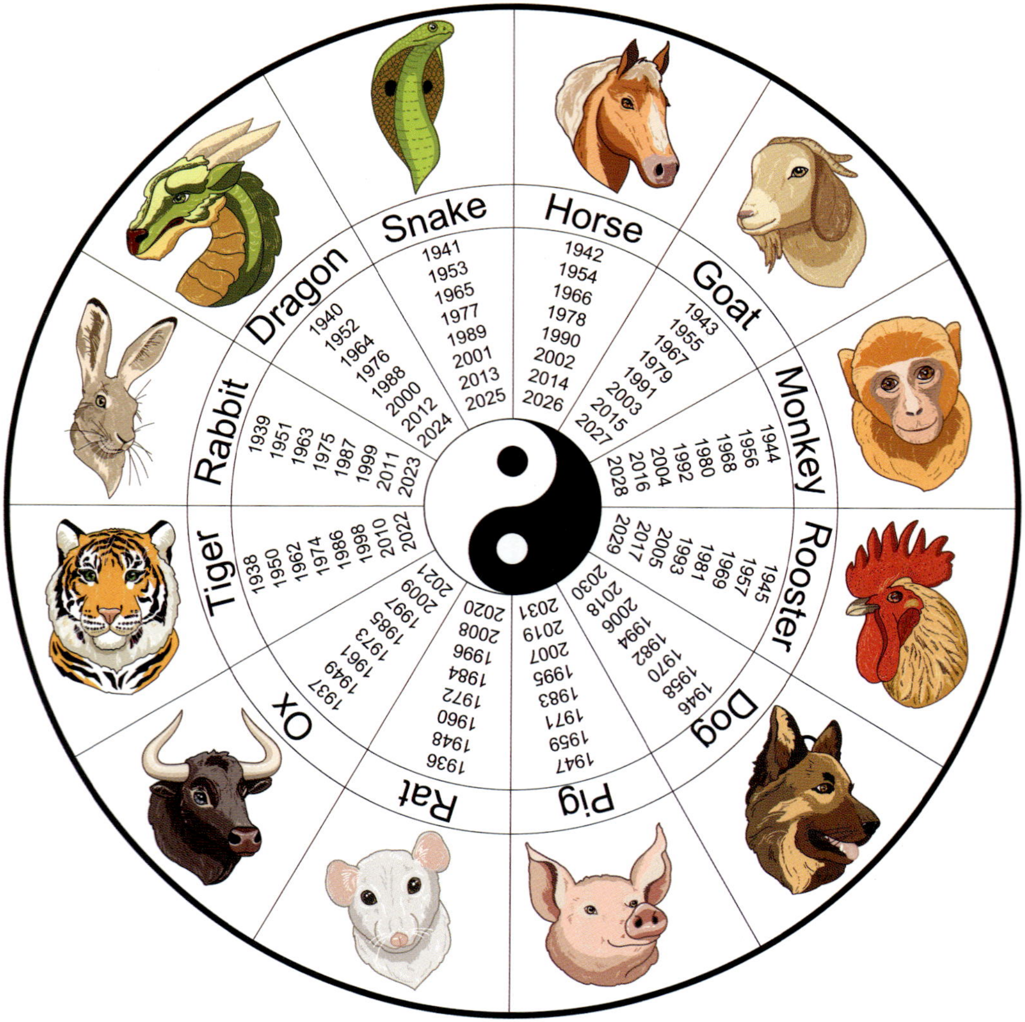

Lunar New Year is one of the biggest holidays in **Asia**. It is celebrated around the world.

HOW TO CELEBRATE

Before the holiday, people get haircuts. They buy new clothes. They clean their homes. They make a fresh start.

Families have **reunions**. They eat moon-shaped **dumplings**. They eat oranges, rice cakes, and other lucky foods.

Red stands for good **fortune**. Kids get *hong bao*. It is money in red envelopes.

There are parades. Dancers with puppets do the lion dance.

The last night is special. It is the **Lantern** Festival. Kids carry glowing lanterns. They solve **riddles** written on the lanterns.

On Lunar New Year, people wish for happiness in the new year.

Everyone feels lucky, and everyone is happy!

GLOSSARY

Asia (AY-zhuh): the world's largest continent

dumplings (DUHMP-lingz): pieces of dough wrapped around fillings and boiled, fried, or steamed

fortune (FOR-chuhn): luck, chance, or wealth

holiday (HAH-li-day): a special day or days; a time when most people do not go to school or work because of a religious or national celebration

lantern (LAN-turn): a kind of lamp; Chinese lanterns have lights inside wood frames covered by paper or fabric

lunar (LOO-nur): related to the moon

reunions (ree-YOON-yuhnz): meetings of people who have not seen each other for a long time

riddles (RID-uhlz): clever questions that make you think hard to find the answer; jokes

THINKING QUESTIONS

1. What decides when Lunar New Year begins?
2. Where is Lunar New Year celebrated?
3. How do people get ready for Lunar New Year?
4. What is *hong bao*?
5. When is the Lantern Festival?

INDEX

ABOUT THE AUTHOR

Kim Thompson lives in Columbus, Ohio, with her husband and two funny cats. She has written many books for kids. Her favorite thing about a new year is the chance to discover new things. Her favorite holiday is the one that is coming up next!